LEARN SONGWRITING

Caroline and Nigel Hooper

Designed by Neil Francis

Edited by Jane Chisholm and Eileen O'Brien

Studio photography by Howard Allman

Managing designer: Steve Wright

Picture researcher: Ruth King

Cover pictures (clockwise from left): Björk, Kurt Cobain, Lauryn Hill, Michael Jackson

CONTENTS

You don't have to be a trained musician to be a good songwriter. Whether you want to learn about writing lyrics (the words), or music, or you simply want to find out how it's done, this book will tell you everything you need to know to get started.

You will find tips to help you with all aspects of songwriting, from the initial idea to the final song, as well as information about how some well-known songs were written. As you read, it will help to try some of the projects suggested.

Later in the book, you can find out about recording your songs, and on page 47 there are addresses to send your songs to.

Songs to listen to

As you learn about each aspect of songwriting, there are suggestions for songs to listen to. Listening to these examples will help you put the things you are learning in context. You can listen to CDs and cassettes free of charge in many record stores, and at public libraries which have a music section. If you have a computer, you can listen to music on the Internet.

Find out how famous songwriters have been inspired to write their songs.

Madonna

There are several elements that make up a song, such as the tune, the lyrics (the words) and the rhythm. Each is equally important to the overall result, but don't be discouraged if you find one thing more difficult than another. Here you will find some helpful advice before you begin.

How to start

There are lots of ways to start writing your own songs. You can start by making up a tune or an accompaniment, or by writing some lyrics. Some people start by thinking of a rhythm. It's a good idea to experiment by starting a different way each time at first. Then find the way that suits you best.

? I can't even play the recorder. How can I write a song if I can't play a musical instrument?

If you want to write the music yourself, you can make up tunes by singing or humming. Remember, though, you don't have to do everything yourself. Many of the best songs are written by more than one person. You might prefer to work on the lyrics, while someone else writes the music.

? I can't even sing. How can I write a song?

Most people will quite happily sing along to songs they like in the privacy of their own homes. Yet many people feel embarrassed to sing in public.

To be a successful songwriter you don't need to be able to sing your songs well enough to perform them. Many of the greatest songwriters write songs for other people to sing.

So, if you can sing in the shower, you can probably sing well enough to make up a song of your own.

PAUL McCARTNEY AND JOHN LENNON

Paul McCartney: *John Lennon:*
Born 1942, UK *Born 1940, UK; Died 1980, U.S.A.*

Paul McCartney (left, in the picture) and John Lennon (right) of The Beatles are widely thought of as two of the greatest songwriters of all time. Yet when The Beatles began in the early 60s, neither Lennon nor McCartney was able to read or write music notation.

? I can play a few chords on a guitar, but I can't read music. How can I write a song if I can't write the music down?

If you can play your song, but don't know how to write it down, you can record it. You don't need a perfect recording at this stage.

If you know someone who can read music, you could ask them to help you write it down. Or, if you know the names of the chords you are playing, you could make a note of the chord names.

It's even possible, using music software, to play your music into a computer on a special keyboard called a midi keyboard, or a midi guitar, and to print the music out. Later in this book there are some tips to help write your music down.

ELTON JOHN AND BERNIE TAUPIN

Elton John:
Born 1947, UK

Bernie Taupin:
Born 1950, UK

Elton John (left, in the picture) and Bernie Taupin (right) have been a very successful songwriting duo for over three decades. With John's popular style of melody writing and Taupin's no-nonsense lyrics, their songs appeal to a huge audience worldwide.

? I couldn't even play the drum at school. How can I write a song if I have no sense of rhythm?

Not everyone is born with a good sense of rhythm, but we all have some natural sense of rhythm, so it is possible to train yourself. Listen to the sounds you hear every day, like the ticking of a clock. This is a rhythm.

Listen to a clock ticking for a while. Try tapping your foot or clapping your hands, or maybe tapping on your knee, every time the clock ticks. If you practice doing this often enough, you can train yourself to keep a steady beat. You could try tapping the beat to some well-known songs for practice.

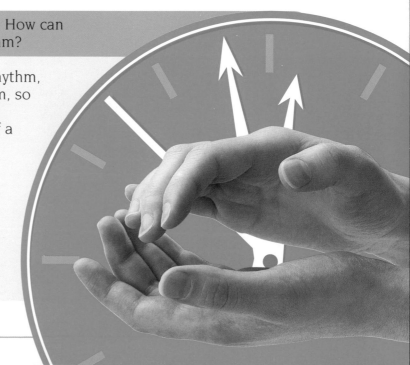

Most songwriters spend a long time thinking of ideas, before developing and fine-tuning them. Occasionally, someone has a flash of inspiration and this turns into a good song. But this is very rare. On these two pages there are some things to consider before you begin.

Dance

Jazz

Rock

Blues

Pop

Musicals

Rap

? What sort of song?

There are many different types of songs, such as blues, pop, rock, rap, songs for musicals and shows, and many more. Before you start, decide which style you are aiming for.

Listen to songs on the radio and television. Think about which styles you like, and notice which ones you find yourself humming or whistling along with.

? Who is your song for?

You may want to learn about songwriting for the fun of it, or just to find out how it all works. If this is the case, you should aim for styles and themes that you like, or are important to you in some way.

If you are considering a career as a songwriter, you should always try to keep the listener in mind. Remember, for a song to be successful, it has to appeal to a large number of people.

BOB DYLAN

Bob Dylan: Born 1941, U.S.A.

During the 60s, Bob Dylan (born Robert Zimmerman) took the popular music scene by storm. With his amazing flair for political lyrics and his folk-style music, Dylan is considered to be one of the most influential songwriters in the world.

When to do it

If you are serious about writing your own songs, it's a good idea to set aside a regular time to work on them. Try to choose a time of day when you are not likely to be disturbed.

Lots of people prefer first thing in the morning, or in the evening, when they are feeling relaxed. Try to avoid times when you are too tired. If you are not concentrating properly, you can forget some of your ideas before you have even had a chance to write them down.

Working on your songs a little each day is sometimes better than working on them for a long time once a week. You are far more likely to remember your train of thought.

Words from a songwriter...

I have trouble with the word "inspiration", because it suggests something just hits you out of the blue... For me, it really is a matter of craft. I sit down when all the other work is done... take the phone off the hook, and I make notes - reams of them.

Brad Roberts (Crash Test Dummies), 1994

Checklist for getting started

- Try to decide upon a style before you start.

- Always keep the listener in mind.

- Pay attention. Listen to the current trends in music on radio and TV. Think carefully about what types of songs you hear most often, and why.

- Don't be discouraged if it seems to take a very long time to come up with any ideas. You have to be patient.

- Try not to be disappointed if your first attempt isn't great. Even the greatest songwriters of all time have probably written more flops than successes.

People often wonder what comes first: the words, or the music? There are many elements that make up a song and any one of them can be the starting point.

Some people start with a tune and then make up some words to go with it. Others start by writing some lyrics, or by making up an accompaniment, or a rhythm. Before you start you need to decide what you want to tackle first.

I'M STROLLING OVER TO JOHN'S COS I JUST DON'T BELONG. SO I THINK HOW IT'S ALL GON START TO I FEEL LIKE I

How to begin

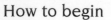

Over the next few pages you can find out about different ways to start writing a song. Reading through these pages should give you some idea of how you want to start. After a while, if it's not working, try another way.

Thing you will need

Apart from time, patience and a little imagination, there is very little you need to begin songwriting. Get yourself a notepad and a pencil, and start taking notice of everything that's going on around you. Keep them with you whenever possible, in case you have any ideas.

Write down key words and subjects as you think of them, and make a note of anything that grabs your attention. Think of some different ways of saying the same thing. Here are some examples:

I'm going to John's house

I'm on my way over to John's place

I'm strolling over to John's

Paul Simon: Born 1942, U.S.A.

Paul Simon wrote many successful songs as part of the duo, Simon and Garfunkel. During the 70s, he embarked on a solo career and began experimenting with music from different cultures. In 1986, he recorded the album *Graceland*, with a group of South African musicians. The album was a huge hit worldwide, and confirmed Simon's ability to fit more words to a tune than most people would even attempt!

PAUL SIMON

What if I think of a tune?

Of course, it's all very well having a notepad and pencil if you think of a word or a subject, but what if you think of a tune? Even people who play a musical instrument often find it difficult to write down music from their head. The trouble is, if you don't write it down, there's a good chance you'll forget it.

If you can't record your song, one thing you can do is to try to draw the shape of the melody. You can do this by drawing a rough line showing where the music goes up and down, or you can try to be a little more accurate and draw a dot for each note. Here's how it's done:

Drawing the shape of a tune

Draw a dot for the first note, then put the next dot higher or lower, depending on whether the tune goes up or down, as shown. Put a separate dot for each note, and leave a larger gap between the dots for longer notes.

If you connect the dots you can see the shape of the melody. It's a little like dot to dot, but it can help you to remember your idea later on. Try drawing the shape of a tune you already know. Look at it a couple of hours later and see if it helps you to relate it to the original tune.

Björk: Born 1966, Iceland

Björk has been involved with music almost all of her life. As a child she frequently sang on Icelandic television, and her experimental songs are now known worldwide.

Songwriter's workshop

- Make up a short phrase. It could be about anything from listening to the radio, to riding on a bus. Try to come up with at least three different ways of saying it.

- Choose two songs. Try to draw the shape of the melody for each of them, as shown on the left. Then compare the shapes to see if there are any similarities.

On the next few pages you can find out about making up a tune, or melody. This is one of the most important parts of a song. People often remember a tune, but not the lyrics. It is far less common for people to remember the lyrics, but not the tune.

Before you start

Before you begin, listen to a few songs in different styles, to help you decide what type of song you want to write. Keep a notepad nearby, to help you remember anything that stands out. Keep this notepad just for songwriting. Don't use it for anything else. Then it will be easier to find things you have written later on. In the checklist on the right, there are some tips to help you.

Checklist

- Listen to a wide variety of songs in different styles before you start.

- Make a note of which songs you like, and which ones you don't. Think carefully about why you like them, or why you don't.

- Try to work out what makes each style sound different. Then decide which styles you like best.

Making up a tune

Many people start to make up a melody by humming, even if they can play a musical instrument. This is a good idea, because the melody needs to be easy to sing. If you are going to use a musical instrument, such as a guitar or keyboard, it is best to hum, or sing, along with it.

Pitch

In music, the word "pitch" describes how high or low the music sounds. If you are writing a song, you have to make sure the tune is at a comfortable pitch to sing. So, the best instrument you can use to write a song is your voice.

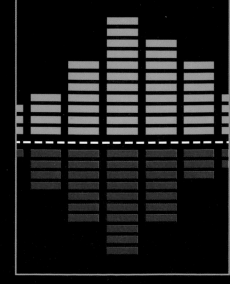

Structure

A good structure will help your song to make sense. To develop a structure, you need to split your song up into sections. The number of sections depends on the type of song you are planning to write.

Sections of a song

A ballad is usually made up of one repeated section, or verse. This is the simplest type of song, and is often used to tell a story.

Verse — **Verse** — **Verse** — **Verse**

The most common type of song is a verse/chorus song, where two different melodic sections, a verse and a chorus, are repeated alternately. You can find out more about the verse and chorus on pages 14 and 15.

Verse — **Chorus** — **Verse** — **Chorus**

Some songs, such as Wonderwall, recorded by Oasis, have a short link between the verse and chorus.

Some songs also have another section, about two thirds of the way through, known as a bridge. This is usually where the song reaches its peak. You can find out more about the bridge on page 18.

Verse — **Chorus** — **Verse** — **Chorus** — **Bridge** — **Chorus**

Stevie Wonder: Born 1950, U.S.A.

Born Steveland Judkins, Stevie Wonder became blind soon after he was born. In spite of this, he learned the piano, drums and harmonica by the age of nine. As he progressed to songwriting, he became a pioneer in the use of synthesizers and music technology.

Words from a songwriter...

I often sit at the piano, working on songs with the television on low in the background. If I'm a bit low and not getting much done, the words from the telly come through. Suddenly I heard the words 'Good morning, good morning'. It was a corn flakes commercial.

John Lennon, 1967, on the song 'Good morning Good morning'

STEVIE WONDER

MUSICAL PHRASES

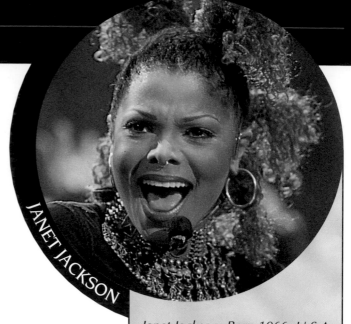

When you talk to someone, the words are grouped together in sentences. In a song, the notes of the melody are grouped together in much the same way. In music, these groups of notes are called phrases. Splitting music up into phrases helps the tune to make sense. It also helps the singer to know where to breathe.

Questions and answers

Sometimes musical phrases are a little like questions and answers. If you stop after the first phrase, the tune does not sound finished. When you play the second phrase, it sounds complete.

Listen to *House Of The Rising Sun*. In this song, the questions and answers are each made up of two phrases. The first two are like a musical question. The next two are like an answer.

Janet Jackson: Born 1966, U.S.A.

Janet Jackson began her stage career at the age of seven, as the youngest member of the 60s and 70s group The Jackson Five. Since launching her solo career, she has co-written many highly successful albums, including *Control* and *Rhythm Nation* 1814.

House Of The Rising Sun

Here is *House Of The Rising Sun* in music notation. Don't worry if you can't read the music. Try to follow the words and look at the shape of the tune.

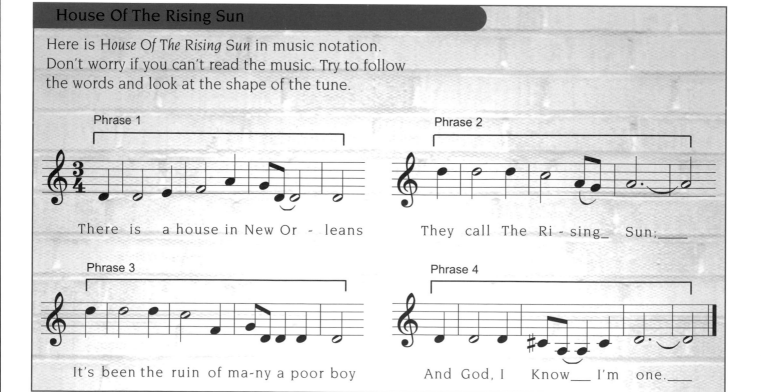

Phrase 1
There is a house in New Or - leans

Phrase 2
They call The Ri - sing_ Sun;____

Phrase 3
It's been the ruin of ma-ny a poor boy

Phrase 4
And God, I Know___ I'm one.____

The shape of the tune

The shape of the melody is very important if you want to hold the listener's attention. Often, the melody gets higher in the middle of the verse, then returns to the original pitch at the end. This happens in *House Of The Rising Sun*.

Another good example of this is in the song *Scarborough Fair*. Each verse of this song is also split up into four melodic phrases. Listen carefully to *Scarborough Fair*, and see if you can work out where each phrase begins. Notice how the melody gradually moves up in pitch over the first two phrases, then comes back down to the original pitch over the last two.

KURT COBAIN

Kurt Cobain: Born 1967, U.S.A.; Died 1994, U.S.A.

Kurt Cobain was the lead singer and guitarist for the American grunge band Nirvana. Though his career with the band was fairly short, his songs continue to be extremely popular, even after his death.

Songs to listen to:

Listen to the shapes of the melodies in these songs:

House Of The Rising Sun,
traditional;
recorded by The Animals

Scarborough Fair,
traditional;
recorded by Simon and Garfunkel

Words from a songwriter...

The first time I came to America I got a notebook, and half the Armed Forces album came from just jotting down things that went past the bus window.

Elvis Costello, 1988

Songwriter's workshop

- Choose two songs you like and listen to the shape of the melodies. It might help to draw the shapes, even just roughly. Try to work out where each phrase begins, and see if you can spot some questions and answers.

- Now make up a melody of your own. Build it up gradually, one phrase at a time. Think about the shape of the tune, and try to make the phrases into questions and answers.

Here you can find out about different sections of a song, such as the verse and chorus, or refrain. There are also some tips on how to develop your tunes.

The verse

While the same melody is used for each verse of a song, the words are usually different. Most songs being with a verse, but some start with the chorus. If you want people to remember your song, it's best to keep the melody of the verse fairly simple. Try to use just one or two ideas, then vary these to complete the tune.

For example, in *House Of The Rising Sun* (see page 12), the first phrase is one idea and the second phrase is another. The third and fourth phrases are variations of these.

The chorus

The words and music of the chorus usually stay the same throughout a song. The chorus should be very simple and very easy to remember.

The hook (see the page opposite) is an important phrase in the song and often appears in the chorus, sometimes repeated several times. The hook often forms either the first or last lines of the chorus, or both. For example, in *Let It Be* by The Beatles the hook is at the start and the end of the chorus.

MADONNA

Madonna: Born 1958, U.S.A.

Madonna trained as a dancer before turning to music, playing drums and singing. Her first hit was a disco track, but she soon developed a more distinctive style, which shot her to international stardom. She went on to write songs for films, such as *Desperately Seeking Susan*, also acting in one of the leading roles.

Words from a songwriter...

If you have a song with a lot of chord changes and musical activity, try to keep the words at a minimum. Otherwise they cancel each other out. The whole experience gets too dense...

Frank Zappa, 1980

The hook

The most important part of your melody is the hook. This is usually the part of a song that people remember more than the rest. The hook can be anything from a vocal or instrumental phrase to a drum beat or just a few notes. It is usually repeated several times throughout a song.

The hook is often the part of the melody that goes with the title or the main subject of your song. For example, in *Layla*, recorded by Derek and the Dominos, the title acts as the hook. Some songs have two hooks, such as *Every Breath You Take*, by The Police. In this, the first hook, the title, is at the beginning of the chorus. The second hook appears at the end of the chorus, with the words "I'll be watching you".

Songs to listen to:

Listen to the hooks in these songs:

Layla,
written by Eric Clapton;
recorded by
Derek and the Dominos

Every Breath You Take,
written by Sting;
recorded by The Police

Let It Be,
written by John Lennon and Paul McCartney;
recorded by The Beatles

Songwriter's workshop

- Imagine you have been asked to write a song. You only have one week to write it, so time is short. The most important thing to work on is a hook. The whole song can revolve around this.

- A good way to start is to think of some titles, or key words. Don't worry too much about the words themselves. You can find out more about writing lyrics and titles later in the book. For now, just get some ideas down on paper.

- Figure out a short section of melody to go with each title. Try to do at least three, if you can.

- Compose three or four variations of this melody for each title. Then try to develop a tune by adding these short sections together. Imagine you are going to repeat the title several times at the start of the chorus, like in *Let It Be*.

ANDREW LLOYD WEBBER

Andrew Lloyd Webber: Born 1948, UK

Andrew Lloyd Webber has been one of the most successful composers of musicals for over 30 years. Often working alongside lyricist Tim Rice, his many hit musicals include *Joseph and the Amazing Technicolor Dreamcoat*, *Jesus Christ Superstar*, *Evita*, *The Phantom of the Opera*, *Cats* and *Starlight Express*. One of the keys to his success is his ability to create simple, easy to remember, hooks.

Here you can learn about different ways to begin and end your song. Both introductions, known as intros, and endings are often based on the hook. This makes a song easy to recognize as soon as you hear it, and easy to remember once it has finished.

Intros are often sung, or played on guitars and keyboards.

Intros

Not all songs have a proper introduction. Some start straightaway with a verse or chorus. Other songs start with an instrumental section or a drum beat. An intro can be useful, though, to set the mood of your song and to make it easy to recognize.

The intro is the first thing the listener will hear, so it needs to grab their attention. You can either have a vocal intro, or an instrumental one. Instrumental introductions, such as the one in *Stairway To Heaven*, by Led Zeppelin, are the most common.

When to add an intro

Intros are often added after the verse and chorus have been written. Sometimes the intro is added even later, during the recording process.

Robbie Williams

Tricks of the trade

There are certain shortcuts you can use to help improve your songs. Intros, for example, can be formed by taking the hook, or a section of the hook, and placing it at the beginning of the song. This is not the same as starting a song with the chorus, as it doesn't necessarily use the whole chorus.

Can't Buy Me Love, by The Beatles, starts in this way. The title, which is the first line of the chorus, and also acts as the hook, is repeated twice at the beginning of the song. This allows the listener to hear the catchiest part of the song first, without giving too much away.

Songwriter's workshop

○ Choose a song you already know, which has an instrumental intro. Write your own vocal intro to the song, basing it on the hook.

○ Next, pick a song which has a vocal intro and make up an intrumental intro to go with it. Base it on an instrumental idea that already appears in the song.

Checklist

• Think about how some of the songs you know start.

• Notice whether the songs you are listening to have instrumental or vocal intros, or whether they start with a drum beat.

• Try to relate the intros of the songs you hear to their hooks.

Endings

Some songs fade out gradually and never really end, while others have a definite ending. If you are recording a song, it is easy to fade the music out when it reaches the end, but this does not always work so well if a song is being performed live.

Songs such as *Fool To Cry*, by The Rolling Stones, work very well fading out. Others, such as *My Way*, sung by Frank Sinatra, have far more impact with a definite ending.

Which ending to use

Which type of ending to use depends very much on the last thing that is heard in your song. This is usually either the chorus, or in the case of a ballad-style song, the end of your verses.

KEITH RICHARDS AND MICK JAGGER

Keith Richards:	Mick Jagger:
Born 1943, UK	Born 1943, UK

Keith Richards (left, in the picture) and Mick Jagger (right) are both members of The Rolling Stones, one of the greatest rock and roll bands of the 60s and 70s. Their highly original material and energetic live shows, appeal to a huge audience.

Songs to listen to:

Stairway To Heaven,
written by
Jimmy Page and Robert Plant;
recorded by
Led Zeppelin

Can't Buy Me Love,
written by
John Lennon and Paul McCartney;
recorded by
The Beatles

Fool To Cry,
written by
Mick Jagger and Keith Richards;
recorded by
The Rolling Stones

My Way,
written by
Revaux, François and Anka;
recorded by
Frank Sinatra

Words from a songwriter...

I like to begin with an idea and then fit it to a title. I then write the words and music. Often I begin near the end of a refrain, so that the song has a strong finish, and then work backwards.

Cole Porter

THE BRIDGE AND THE BREAK

Apart from the verse and chorus, some songs have other sections, called the bridge and the break. A bridge is a vocal section which uses a different tune from the verse and chorus. A break is an instrumental section, usually based around the melody or chords of a song.

The break

The break usually occurs near the middle of a song and allows a diversion from the main theme. Breaks were very common in the 60s and 70s. An example of a 60s break is the one in *Light My Fire*, by The Doors. Sometimes a break is used instead of a bridge.

The break is often put in at a later stage, in the recording studio, for example. It is usually added by a member of the band, or the producer.

Breaks are often played on guitar, keyboards, drums and saxophone.

The bridge

A bridge can help to add variety to a song. It also allows you to build the melody up to a climax, or change the mood of your song. This is especially useful for songs which have no chorus, such as *Memories* from the hit musical *Cats*, by Andrew Lloyd Webber. A bridge is sometimes used in verse/chorus songs as well.

Jimi Hendrix:
Born 1942, U.S.A.; Died 1970, UK

Jimi Hendrix began teaching himself the guitar at the age of twelve. Most of the ideas for his songs came from jamming sessions with other musicians, or by experimenting on his guitar in a studio. Apart from writing his own songs, Hendrix is also renowned for his arrangements of other people's songs, particularly his stunning version of Bob Dylan's *All Along The Watchtower*.

Songs to listen to:

Listen to the bridge in this song:

Memories,
written by
Andrew Lloyd Webber,
T. S. Eliot
and Don Black;
from the musical Cats

Listen to the break in this song:

Light My Fire,
written by
Robby Krieger;
recorded by The Doors

JIMI HENDRIX

? When should I use a bridge or a break?

It's not always necessary to have a bridge or a break, so don't try to force one into your songs. Only use one if a song seems to require it. Remember that a bridge or a break is especially useful for songs that have no chorus. It's also good for songs that use lots of melodic repetition, as it provides some variety.

Songwriter's workshop

● Using some of the ideas you have come up with so far, work out a structure for a song. Don't worry about the lyrics just yet. For now, concentrate mostly on the tune.

● Remember, only include a bridge or break section if it feels natural to have one.

● When you have come up with a melody, or phrase, build up the rest of the tune around it. You could do this by changing the order of the notes slightly, or by using the shape of the melody at a higher pitch.

CAROLE KING

Checklist

• Try out lots of ideas. The more you try, the more fun songwriting becomes.

• Think about how often you can repeat a phrase before it becomes boring. Be careful though. Too much variety can make your tune difficult to remember.

• Try to express some strong feelings in your tunes. What makes a cheerful tune sound different from a sad tune?

Carole King: Born 1942, U.S.A.

Carole King carved out a successful career in songwriting during the 60s, alongside Gerry Goffin (born 1939, U.S.A.), with hits such as *Locomotion* and *One Fine Day*. Because of the universal appeal of her songs, numerous covers have appeared over the years. Ella Fitzgerald, James Taylor, Barbra Streisand, Michael Jackson and Don Williams are among the many artists who have recorded *You've Got A Friend*.

Over the next few pages you can find out how to go about writing lyrics. If you don't play a musical instrument, this can be a good place to start.

How to begin

Most people start by jotting down lots of words, or ideas. Some start by thinking of a title, or a key phrase. Another way to begin is to choose a subject, then make a note of any words or phrases you can think of to do with that subject.

If you don't have a particular subject in mind for your song, you could start by writing down anything that comes into your head. Then pick out some words and phrases you like and try to build your lyrics around them.

Thinking of ideas

You can get ideas for lyrics from almost anywhere. Look around you. Write down everything you can see. This will give you some words to start off with. Listen to things people say, especially when they're in a hurry. You can often get some good one-liners from this.

field

cows

milk

cream

strawberry

fruit

?

Can you think of some more words?

Tricks of the trade

Once you have written some words, you can use word association to expand on them. The easiest way to do this is in the form of a word tree, like the one on these two pages.

Who knows, this could have been the starting point for *Strawberry Fields Forever*, or *Yellow Submarine*, by Lennon and McCartney.

Checklist

• It's a good idea to keep a notepad and pencil with you, in case you have any ideas for songs. Write down anything interesting you see or hear. Remember, you can develop what you have written down later.

• Listen to lots of songs. Notice how the lyrics work. Think about which words rhyme and which ones don't.

• Above all, be patient. Don't expect to come up with something good in five minutes.

David Bowie: Born 1947, UK

David Bowie is known almost as much for his outlandish stage shows as for his unique style of singing and songwriting. His often bizarre lyrics were, in fact, sometimes literally worked out by picking a series of words out of a hat.

- ?
- yellow
- skin
- **Banana**
- boat
- slip
- ?
- water
- sea
- submarine

Songs to listen to:

Listen to the lyrics here:

Strawberry Fields Forever,
written by John Lennon and Paul McCartney; *recorded by* The Beatles

Yellow Submarine,
written by John Lennon and Paul McCartney; *recorded by* The Beatles

Songwriter's workshop

○ Next time you go out, make a conscious effort to notice what's going on around you. When you get back home, try to remember as much as you can, and make a note of anything you found interesting.

○ Choose a word and make your own word association tree. Try to have at least three branches, to give you a wide variety of words.

21

In the same way that your melody needs to have some sort of structure, so do your lyrics. Although you may start by writing down a jumble of words, once you begin to write full lines and phrases, you need to think about organizing them into sections.

Organizing your lyrics

Try to build up a framework by deciding how many lines you are going to have in each verse, for example, and whether or not you are going to have a chorus. As the framework progresses, decide whether it is appropriate to include a bridge section.

What is your song about?

Probably the most popular subject to write about is love, but there are many other good themes you can use. Common subjects include money, work, politics, friendship, philosophy, a particular place or event, and many more. Some songs use nonsense words, or words that make little sense, such as *Dedododo Dedadada*, by The Police.

If you have already written a melody, think about what sorts of subjects might go well with it. You may even have had some ideas while working on the melody of your song.

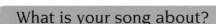

The Artist: Born 1958, U.S.A.

Born Prince Rogers Nelson, The Artist (formerly known as Prince) was one of the most creative, yet controversial, songwriters of the 80s and 90s. Albums such as *Sign O' the Times* released in 1987, show his ability to combine styles such as pop, funk, rock, and rhythm and blues.

What to call your song

A good song needs a good title. Many songwriters begin by thinking of a title. The most simple kind is one that tells us the subject of the song in one or two words, such as *Respect*, by Otis Redding, or *Beat It*, by Michael Jackson.

Some titles are in the form of a statement, such as *Don't Go Breaking My Heart*, by Elton John and Bernie Taupin. Others form a question, for example, *Will You Love Me Tomorrow?*, by Gerry Goffin and Carole King.

If the title is also the hook of your song, you need to find a title that fits with your melody. Titles that are repeated several times throughout a song are far easier to remember.

Exceptions

Not all titles act as the hook. In fact, some titles don't appear anywhere in the song, for example, *Space Oddity*, by David Bowie. Be careful about not including the title in your song though. Your listeners may not remember it.

Songs to listens to:

Listen to how the titles are used in these songs:

Respect,
written by Otis Redding;
recorded by Aretha Franklin

Don't Go Breaking My Heart,
written by Elton John and Bernie Taupin;
recorded by Elton John and Kiki Dee

Will You Love Me Tomorrow?,
written by Gerry Goffin and Carole King;
recorded by The Shirelles

Beat It,
written and recorded by Michael Jackson

Space Oddity,
written and recorded by David Bowie

Checklist

- Don't confuse writing lyrics with writing poetry. A poem is something you ponder, whereas lyrics need to be far more direct.

- Avoid making the listener think about what something means. It is better to make it obvious.

- If possible, try to write about something people would be interested in. Don't make the listener think "So what?".

Songwriter's workshop

- Make a list of common subjects in your songwriting notebook. Use the subjects as headings and set aside at least two pages for each subject. Then, write down as many words or phrases as you can think of to do with that subject.

- You can add to these pages whenever you think of a useful word or phrase. This can be an invaluable source of reference later on.

Here you can find out about the difference between writing lyrics for a verse and a chorus.

The verse

The verse is the part of a song that tells the story. Most songs have no more than four verses, and often this includes repeating the first verse at the end of the song. This doesn't give you very long to tell your story, so your lyrics need to be clear and easy to understand. If your audience has to work too hard at understanding what you mean, they might not bother to try.

The first verse usually sets the scene or mood of a song. This is where the subject and characters are introduced, so it's important to decide whose point of view you are speaking from. Is the singer acting as a narrator, or as one of the characters, or simply as an onlooker? Whichever you decide, try to stick to it throughout the song, or the story may become confusing.

A new point of view

If you do change the point of view, make sure you tell the listener. There are several ways of doing this, but don't be afraid of the obvious. The words "She said...", or "He cried..." are sufficient to let your listener know there is a change. A good example of this is The Boomtown Rats' hit I *Don't Like Mondays*. Listen to some other songs and see if you can spot how other people get around this.

The chorus

The chorus is the part of your song that you want people to go away singing, or humming. It is usually repeated two or three times. Many songs end by repeating the chorus and then gradually fading out. Usually the chorus revolves around the hook of the song. This can be the title, or a word or phrase that sums up the subject, such as *Dancing Queen*, by Abba, or I *Just Called To Say I Love You*, by Stevie Wonder.

KURT WEILL

Kurt Weill:
Born 1900, Germany; Died 1950, U.S.A.
Composer and songwriter Kurt Weill wrote several songs which are revived on a regular basis. These include classics such as *Mack The Knife*, performed by Frank Sinatra, *September Song*, sung by a variety of artists including Bing Crosby and Frank Sinatra, and *Alabama Song*, later revived by the Doors and David Bowie.

The hook

The hook is perhaps the most important part of your song, whether you are writing a melody, or lyrics. Think of at least two songs you like. Notice how easily you can identify them from the hook. No matter how good your song is, there needs to be one part that sticks in peoples' minds more than the rest.

Tricks of the trade

Try to repeat the hook several times during your song. If the hook is in the chorus of your song, you could repeat it several times within the chorus. This is a popular trick and is used in many famous songs. Listen to the hooks in *Lola*, by the Kinks, and *We Are The Champions*, by Queen.

Developing the hook

A good hook can be the difference between the success or failure of a song, so you need to spend a lot of time experimenting. Many songwriters change the words in the hook several times before deciding which works best and which is the most catchy.

During the 80s, for example, the American singer-songwriter Billy Ocean had a big hit with the song *Caribbean Queen*. This song had previously been released by him as *African Queen* and then *European Queen*, but with little success. Changing a single word in the verses, chorus, or any other part of a song may not make much difference, but changing a word in the hook can make a huge difference to the song.

STING

Sting: Born 1951, UK

Born Gordon Sumner, Sting first made his name as a respected singer-songwriter with the band The Police, writing hits such as *Message in a Bottle*. As a solo artist, he continues to write catchy pop songs, often with elements of jazz.

Songs to listen to:

Listen to the hooks in these songs:

Dancing Queen,
written by Benny Andersson and Björn Ulvaeus;
recorded by Abba

I Just Called To Say I Love You,
written and recorded by Stevie Wonder

Caribbean Queen,
written and recorded by Billy Ocean

Lola,
written by Ray Davis;
recorded by The Kinks

We Are The Champions,
written by Freddie Mercury;
recorded by Queen

Notice how the point of view changes in this song:

I Don't Like Mondays,
written by Bob Geldof;
recorded by The Boomtown Rats

Songwriter's workshop

○ Imagine you have to write a song in a hurry. It needs to be catchy, so begin with the chorus. Try to come up with four hooks, and develop a chorus from each of them. Remember to repeat the hook at least two or three times.

Most songs use some sort of rhyme pattern. This is called a rhyme scheme. Think about how many nursery rhymes you can remember from your childhood. One of the reasons you can remember them is that they have an obvious rhyme scheme.

Should your lyrics rhyme?

Songs that rhyme are generally far easier to remember. Rhymes also help to give your song a pattern and make it sound more balanced. This can help when you are making up a tune to go with your lyrics.

Different types of rhyme

There are lots of different types of rhymes and many ways of using them. For instance, in some songs, the first and second lines rhyme, whereas in others the first and third lines rhyme. Some words sound almost the same, such as 'found' and 'round'; others sound fairly similar, but do not rhyme exactly, such as 'found' and 'down'.

Many songwriters use rhyming dictionaries, which give lists of rhyming words. These can be useful if you are stuck for a word which rhymes. You can learn about different types of rhymes on the page opposite.

Little Miss Muffet

Little Miss Muffet
Sat on a tuffet,
Eating her curds and whey;
Along came a spider,
Who sat down beside her,
And frightened Miss Muffet away.

In the nursery rhyme, Little Miss Muffet, the first and second lines rhyme.

Simple Simon

Simple Simon met a pieman
Going to the fair;
Said Simon to the pieman,
"Let me taste your ware".

Said the Pieman unto Simon,
"Show me first your penny";
Said Simple Simon to the pieman,
"Sir, I haven't any".

In Simple Simon, the first and third lines rhyme.

CHARLES TRENET

Charles Trenet: Born 1913, France

French-born singer and songwriter Charles Trenet has written many songs which are popular throughout the Western world. Although some of his songs, such as *La Mer*, have been translated into English (as *Beyond the Sea*), most are more widely known in their original language. One of the reasons for this success is that, despite many people being unable to understand the words, the patterns of rhymes are usually very distinct.

True rhymes

True, or perfect, rhymes are those where both words have the same sound, so they rhyme exactly. For example, 'mine' and 'line', 'hear' and 'fear', 'gold' and 'hold' are all true rhymes.

Make a list of all the true rhymes you can think of. You can add to this whenever you think of another. Lists like this are a good point of reference when you are writing lyrics, and can save you a lot of time.

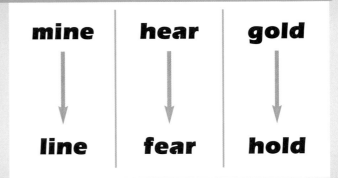

False rhymes

When two words sound similar, but not the same, these are known as false rhymes, or half rhymes. For example, 'once' and 'dance', 'half' and 'life', 'town' and 'ground' are all false rhymes. When you are writing lyrics, sometimes it is more appropriate to use a word which has the right meaning, even though it doesn't quite rhyme. These sorts of rhymes are very common in popular music. Try to think of some more false rhymes to go with the words on the right.

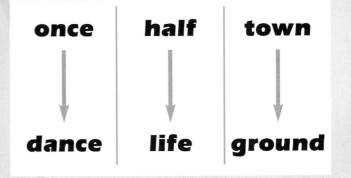

Songwriter's workshop

● Try writing two verses of a song, one using true rhymes and one using false rhymes. They don't have to go together as part of the same song, so don't worry about keeping the same subject.

● In the first verse of the song, end the first and second lines with words that rhyme, and end the third and fourth lines with words that rhyme.

● In the other verse, end the first and third lines with words that rhyme, and end the second and fourth lines with words that rhyme.

Songs to listen to:

Listen to the rhyme schemes in the following songs:

Heard It Through The Grapevine,
written by
Holland, Dozier, Holland;
recorded by Marvin Gaye

Love Me Tender,
written by Matson and Presley;
recorded by Elvis Presley

Seasons In The Sun,
written by Jacques Brel;
recorded by Terry Jacks

La Mer,
written and recorded by
Charles Trenet

There are several different ways to use rhymes in your songs. Once you have begun to write some lyrics, a pattern will start to develop, and then you can decide the best places to use a rhyme. Here is some more advice to help you.

Multi-syllable rhymes

Multi-syllable rhymes are rhymes using words which have more than one syllable. Sometimes only the last syllable rhymes, such as in 'younger' and 'brighter', and sometimes the last two syllables rhyme, such as in 'degrading' and 'parading'. It is also possible to have more than two syllables that rhyme, for example, 'vocation' and 'location', but these are usually less common.

Rhymes using words with three or more syllables are often false rhymes. Longer words can help to give your song a natural rhythm, though, so don't dismiss them.

younger

brighter

degrading

parading

vocation

location

Open and closed rhymes

A closed rhyme uses words that end with a hard letter, such as 'd' or 'k'. An open rhyme uses words that don't end with a hard letter, such as 'go' and 'slow', or 'stay' and 'way'. You should try to use open rhymes whenever a note in the melody is likely to be held for any length of time.

Closed rhymes, such as 'mad' and 'bad', or 'back' and 'pack', are better used in places where the note is not likely to be held. If possible, you should also try to avoid using words that end in an 's' at the end of a line. This can produce a hissing sound, especially on a recording.

go

slow

stay

way

mad

bad

Songwriter's workshop

- Make up a melody for a verse of a song. Then add some lyrics, taking particular care over the words you use at the end of each line. Think carefully about open and closed rhymes, and which words go with which parts of the melody.

- Perhaps you could get together with a friend. Try contributing alternate lines and see where it leads you. This can sometimes help to add a relaxed, conversational feeling to your lyrics. It's also a good way to help you get started.

- Now write some lyrics for a second verse, using the same rhyme pattern that you used for the first verse.

Simple rhyme patterns

In the most simple rhyme pattern, the last word of the first and third lines rhyme with each other, and the last word of the second and fourth lines rhyme with each other. For example, *The Name of the Game*, by Abba, uses this rhyme pattern.

In some songs, the first and second lines end with a word that rhymes, then the third and fourth lines end with a word that rhymes. This type of rhyme scheme is used in *The Sound Of Silence*, by Simon and Garfunkel. Try to find more songs that use these patterns.

Other rhyme patterns

Some songs use more complicated rhyme patterns than the ones discussed on the left. For instance, in the song *Morning Has Broken* there are rhymes in the middle of each line, as well as at the end. This type of rhyme pattern is fairly difficult to write, but it is a very clever way of making your lyrics easy to remember. Be careful, though. If you try to force too many words to rhyme, your lyrics might end up making less sense. You want the listener to be able to understand what you are trying to say.

Songs to listen to:

Listen to the rhyme patterns in the following songs:

The Name of the Game,
written by Anderson, Andersson and Ulvaeus; *recorded by* Abba

The Sound Of Silence,
written by Paul Simon; *recorded by* Simon and Garfunkel

Morning Has Broken,
traditional; *recorded by* Cat Stevens

ABBA

Benny Andersson: Born 1946, Sweden
Björn Ulvaeus: Born 1945, Sweden

Benny Andersson (second from the left in the picture) and Björn Ulvaeus (far right) were members of Abba, one of the most successful groups of the 70s. As the group's songwriters, they wrote one hit after another until the group split up in the early 80s. Later, they teamed up with Tim Rice (see page 15) to write the hit musical *Chess*. Their songs were so popular that, during the 90s, a group called Björn Again formed to imitate their style.

Some songs are accompanied by chords played on a musical instrument such as a guitar or keyboard. A chord is a group of two or more notes, played at the same time. Other songs are accompanied by lots of different instruments, such as stringed or brass instruments. Some songs have more complicated electronic, or synthesized, accompaniments.

NOEL GALLAGHER

Noel Gallagher: Born 1967, UK

Noel Gallagher, songwriter and guitarist for the British band Oasis, is widely acknowledged as one of the best songwriters of the 90s. Albums such as *Definitely Maybe*, released in 1994, are heavily influenced by The Beatles.

How to begin

Whatever type of accompaniment you have in mind for your song, it is best to begin by working out some chords that fit with your melody. If you want a more sophisticated accompaniment, you can develop this later, based on these chords. For example, string and brass sections are usually added in a recording studio.

Starting with an accompaniment

If you play a musical instrument, such as the guitar or keyboard, you may want to start writing your song by working out a sequence of chords. There are some suggestions for chords that go well together at the end of this book.

When you have made up a chord sequence, try recording it, then play it back and improvise some tunes while you listen to it. If you are confident at playing the chords, you could hum along to them to find a tune that fits.

How to play chords

Even if you don't play an instrument, if you have access to a guitar or keyboard you could try playing chords yourself. You don't have to be able to read music. At the end of this book, there are some diagrams to show you how to play the most common chords on a guitar or keyboard.

You may find it difficult to play chords at first, but it does become easier with practice. Some keyboards have an auto-accompaniment feature, so you don't even have to play the chords yourself.

Adding an accompaniment

Although some songs start out as a sequence of chords, most accompaniments are added after the melody has been written. Often, the accompaniment is added in the recording studio, by a producer or arranger.

When you are adding an accompaniment, above all, keep it simple. Start by finding notes which sound good with the melody, to help you work out which chords sound best. Bear in mind, you don't need to play a separate chord for each note of the melody. You can create an accompaniment using only three different chords. On pages 43 and 45 you can find out which groups of three chords to play together.

Songwriter's workshop

○ Learn to play a three-chord sequence on a keyboard or guitar (see pages 43 and 45). Being able to play a few basic chords on a guitar or keyboard is very useful, especially if you want to continue to improve your songwriting skills.

○ You probably know someone who has one of these instruments. If you don't, you could ask a local school or college for permission to use one of theirs. Alternatively you can rent instruments on a short-term basis from most music stores, for a small fee.

Burt Bacharach:
Born 1928, U.S.A.

Composer Burt Bacharach wrote a huge number of successful songs for a variety of different artists. Bacharach frequently worked as part of a team with lyricist Hal David (born 1921). Songs from the 60s such as *Walk On By* were so popular they are still being covered by contemporary performers.

Songs to listen to:

Listen to the accompaniments in the following songs:

Don't look back in anger, *written by* Noel Gallagher; *recorded by* Oasis

Walk On By, *written by* Bacharach and David; *recorded by* Dionne Warwick

Checklist

• Do you want a full-sounding accompaniment or a gentle, lilting sound? A full-sounding accompaniment can add atmosphere to your song, especially if you build up to a climax at a key point in the song, but it's not always appropriate.

• Spend lots of time experimenting. Record your results and listen to them several times to help you decide what works and what doesn't.

• Try experimenting with the rhythm. Remember, the rhythm of the accompaniment does not have to follow that of the tune. It can be effective to have a contrast.

BURT BACHARACH

The rhythm of your song is what holds everything together. The rhythm can be dictated by the melody, or the accompaniment, or even the lyrics, but it is usually assisted by drums and a bass guitar, or a computerized drum machine (see the opposite page). A catchy rhythm can add an extra hook to your song, and make it appeal to a wider audience. You can experiment with different rhythms by tapping on your knee, or on a table, while you hum the tune.

SHERYL CROW

The rhythmic hook

It is just as important to have a good rhythm for the hook of your song as it is to have a catchy tune and memorable words. Some songwriters, such as Cole Porter and Paul Simon, began many of their songs by working out a background rhythm.

You don't have to work out the rhythm for the whole song. You could just think of a short, catchy rhythm which you could use as the basis for your background rhythm. Bear in mind that a catchy rhythm will be easy to remember, and can get people moving to the beat of the music, regardless of the words or tune. Think of dance tracks, for instance.

Getting ideas

Listen to the sounds around you, first in a fairly quiet place, and then in a town, or a busy store. *Money*, by Pink Floyd, and *Driving In My Car*, by Madness, are excellent examples of how a rhythm can be created using familiar sounds. In *Money*, the rhythm uses the sound of cash registers being opened and closed. *Driving In My Car* uses car horns. In both songs, the rhythm acts as a hook.

Sheryl Crow: Born 1962, U.S.A.

Sheryl Crow was already a successful songwriter before achieving fame as a singer, and her songs have been recorded by artists such as Bette Midler. Despite taking almost a year to make an impact, her debut album *Tuesday Night Music Club* was eventually a huge success. Catchy rhythms play a large part in the popularity of her songs.

Songs to listen to:

Listen to the background rhythms in the following songs:

Money,
written by Roger Waters;
recorded by Pink Floyd

Driving In My Car,
written by Michael Barson;
recorded by Madness

Adding a rhythm part

The background rhythm is often added at a later stage, either by the band during rehearsals, or in a recording studio. Adding the rhythm part can help your song to make sense. The speed and style of the background rhythm can also help to create the mood of a song, for example, by being lively or gentle, smooth or spiky.

Drum machines

In a recording studio, the rhythm part is often added using a drum machine. This is an electronic device that produces a computerized drum beat which can be speeded up or slowed down. It can also be altered by adding or taking away extra layers of drum beats.

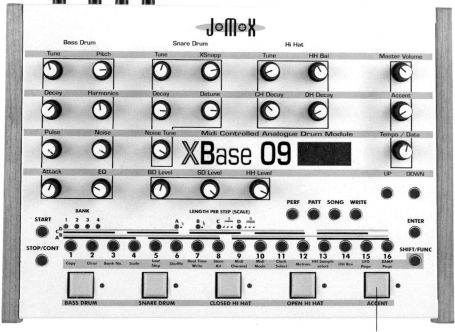

You can choose sounds and play rhythms on this drum machine by tapping on the pads.

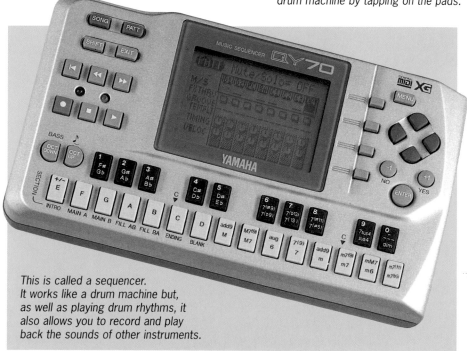

This is called a sequencer. It works like a drum machine but, as well as playing drum rhythms, it also allows you to record and play back the sounds of other instruments.

Spoken words have a rhythm of their own. For example, one syllable in a word may be stressed more than the others. In a sentence, short or less important words may be spoken faster than longer or more important ones. Often the meaning changes depending on which word you stress. For example, "Can I go?" has a different meaning depending on whether you stress the word "I" or "go".

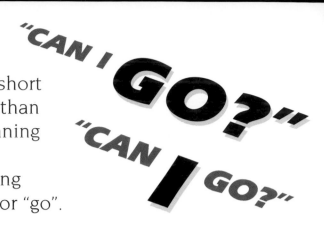

The beat

When you listen to songs, you often find yourself moving to the music in some way, such as tapping your foot. What you are doing is tapping out the regular pulse of the music, known as the beat. In music, the beat holds everything together. The mood and style of a song can be completely changed simply by altering the speed or volume of the beat.

Making words stand out

Beats in music are usually grouped in sets of two, three, or four. Each group is called a bar. The first beat in each bar is usually stressed more than the others, so words sung on this beat will stand out more.

In the examples on the right, there are two beats in each bar. Each clap is one beat. The bars are separated by lines. Clap, or tap out, the beats and say the words beside them. Clap a little louder for the first beat of each bar. Can you hear how the meaning changes, depending on which words are stressed?

clap	
clap	**Can**
clap	**I**
clap	**go?**
clap	
clap	
clap	
clap	
clap	**Can**
clap	**I**
clap	**go?**
clap	

Which words to stress

Try saying your lyrics out loud, and notice which words are stressed during normal speech. This will give you a good idea of the words that need to be stressed in the music. It will also help you to figure out how many beats are in each bar. You need to know this to develop a background rhythm.

May - be   I   just
clap clap clap clap
thought I   knew   it
clap   clap   clap   clap

Songwriter's workshop

○ Next time you are listening to some music, tap out the beat. See if you can determine how many beats are in each bar. Listen out for words that are stressed more than others, to help you decide.

○ Choose some lyrics you have already written. By saying them out loud, try to work out a regular pattern of beats. Then, experiment with putting the stress on different words. Notice the effect this has on them.

Songs to listens to:

Listen to these songs and try to figure out how many beats are in a bar:

Money, Money, Money,
written by
Björn Ulvaeus and
Benny Andersson;
recorded by
Abba

(Sittin' On) The Dock Of The Bay,
written by
Cropper and Redding;
recorded by
Otis Redding

JACQUES BREL

Jacques Brel: Born 1929, Belgium; Died 1978, Belgium

Belgian singer-songwriter Jacques Brel is one of the few Europeans to have a substantial amount of his work translated into English. Songs such as *Le Moribond* sold over a million copies as *Seasons In The Sun*, its translation. His songs have been recorded by a variety of artists, including Frank Sinatra and David Bowie.

The way you present your songs can make a huge difference as to whether or not they are going to be successful. Bear in mind that talent scouts employed by record companies will generally only listen to the first 30 to 60 seconds of a song. Your song has to make an immediate impression.

The performer

If you don't intend to sing your songs yourself, you could try to find out about local bands. You can do this by looking through your local newspaper, or by searching on the Internet. Try to find out what kind of music they play, and whether or not they write their own material. Ask them if they would be interested in trying out some of your songs. You could even place your own advertisement in a local newspaper.

Choosing a performer

The performer you choose could help to sell your song, so don't be afraid to audition people. This can be great fun, and it's interesting to hear different interpretations of your song. Try to choose a band, or singer, whose style suits your songs.

Michael Jackson:
Born 1958, U.S.A.

Michael Jackson became a worldwide success from the age of six, with his unique vocal style and, later, his innovative choreography. When released in 1982, his album *Thriller* was the biggest selling album to date. Six of the nine tracks, including *Billie Jean* and *The Girl is Mine*, became hits independently of the album, and the song *Beat It* sold over a million copies. Much of the success of Jackson's songs is due to the energy he puts into their performance.

MICHAEL JACKSON

A lead sheet is a piece of paper showing the basic outline of a song. It usually contains the melody line, the lyrics, and symbols above the music to indicate which chords to use. It also shows the title, the name of the songwriter and lyricist, and the year the song was written. Here you can see what a lead sheet looks like.

Why do I need a lead sheet?

A lead sheet is useful for two reasons. Firstly, it is helpful for anyone wanting to sing your song, for example, if you are planning to hold auditions. Perhaps most importantly, though, it is a written record of your song and when it was composed. This is very important for copyright purposes (see page 41).

Always write who the words are by, as well as the music.

It is a good idea to indicate the general speed and style of the song, eg. medium rock, or slow blues.

These letters show which chords to play and when to play them. You can find out more about chord symbols on page 45.

Songwriter's workshop

○ On pages 42 to 45, there are some charts showing all the notes on a guitar and keyboard, and how they are written in music notation. On page 46 there is also a guide to writing rhythms.

○ Find the first note of one of your songs by experimenting on a guitar or keyboard. Use the charts at the end of the book to help you write it down in music notation.

○ Continue with the rest of the melody. Use the guide on page 46 to help you with the rhythm. Gradually try to write out a lead sheet. This is quite difficult, so don't worry if it takes a long time.

RECORDING YOUR SONGS

If you want a record company to give your songs a fair hearing, you need to send a good quality recording. A poor quality recording will probably be switched off in seconds, so it's a good idea to hire a recording studio. You can find out about studios for hire in music magazines, or on the Internet, and some further education colleges have facilities they may allow you to use. Prices vary from one studio to another, so shop around.

RECORDING STUDIO

The producer

The producer is the person who puts your song together in the studio. Most studios have a producer, or engineer, whom you can hire with the studio. A good producer can literally transform your song.

Arrangements

The arrangement of a song is how it is all put together. This is often the stage at which you add your rhythm and accompaniment sections, and other things such as intros and instrumental breaks.

Many songs are arranged in a recording studio, either by the artist or songwriter, or the producer. The equipment in studios is geared to this, so you can experiment with adding strings or brass sounds, and backing vocals. It's a good idea to decide roughly what you want beforehand, though, as studio time can be quite expensive.

Building a song track by track

In a recording studio, a song is built up gradually, layer by layer. Each layer is called a track. The first track that is recorded is a drum track, to provide a steady beat. Often several different drum tracks are recorded. These are then put together (or "mixed") to make the background rhythm sound more interesting.

Usually the next track to be recorded consists of chords, normally played on a keyboard. Sometimes two keyboard tracks are recorded to give the sound more depth. Then the guitar parts and backing vocals are added, and any orchestral parts. Usually the lead vocals are the last thing you record.

Drums

Keyboard

Guitar

Backing vocals

Orchestra

Lead vocals

Tricks of the trade

To add fullness to the overall sound, some people record the same section of vocals several times, then mix them all together. Although the same thing is being recorded, it is bound to be slightly different each time it is sung. When two or more of these tracks are heard at the same time, it creates a fuller sound.

Technology

It is possible, using computer software, to create a song in as little as half an hour. Many dance tracks are created in this way, using techniques such as sampling. Sampling is where sounds are recorded and then altered, for example, by being stopped in mid-flow, or repeated several times very quickly.

Using other songs

Sometimes songs that already exist are sampled to form part of a new song. This means that you can base your song around a hook that is already proved to be successful. Janet Jackson's *Got 'Til It's Gone*, for example, is based on the Joni Mitchell track *Big Yellow Taxi*.

If you want to try this, you must get permission from whoever owns the copyright for that song. The record company should be able to give you this information. You will then need to pay royalties to the owner. A royalty is a percentage of the price a CD is sold for in the stores.

You also need to get permission to perform someone else's song in public. You can find out about performance royalties on page 41.

Songs to listen to:

Listen to how part of the first song here is sampled in the second:

Big Yellow Taxi,
written and recorded by
Joni Mitchell

Got 'Til It's Gone,
written by
Elizondo, Fareed, Harris, Jackson, Lewis, Mitchell;
recorded by
Janet Jackson

Public domain music

Alternatively, you can base a song on public domain music. This is music which is out of copyright, so there are no royalties to pay. You can find out if a piece of music is public domain by contacting the Performing Rights Society in the UK, and companies such as Broadcast Music Inc. in the U.S. (see page 47 for the addresses).

GEORGE MARTIN

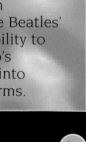

*George Martin:
Born 1926, UK*

George Martin became the world's most famous record producer through his work with The Beatles. In fact, he is often referred to as "the fifth Beatle". A classically trained musician, his main contribution to the Beatles' music lay in his ability to translate the group's adventurous ideas into practical musical terms.

Once you have a demo tape, or CD, you can start trying to sell your songs. This is not easy. You will need to be very determined and very patient, but on these two pages there are some tips to help you go about it. On page 47 there are some useful addresses you may want to send your songs to.

Managers

A manager can help to market your songs. He or she can also help to negotiate contracts and fees, as well as trying to promote your work to record companies. In fact, it's very rare for a performer or songwriter to secure a recording deal without a good manager.

The best way to find a manager is by asking around. Get in touch with D.J.s, booking agents, club owners and local bands. They are in a good position to know who works in your area and, more importantly, who is good. Try to have any management contracts or agreements looked over by a music business lawyer before you sign them.

Agents

Having your songs performed live is a good way of getting yourself noticed by record company talent scouts. If you, or the band performing your songs, don't play regularly, it's a good idea to hire an agent. It is the responsibility of an agent to organize gigs and to make sure they are well advertised. Your manager, local bands or club owners might have ideas about which agent to choose. Make sure, however, that the agent is someone who is enthusiastic about your music.

Registering your song

It is important to register your song in some way, in order to prove that you wrote it. It is better to do this legally, either through a solicitor, or through the copyright registry at Stationers Hall in the UK, or the United States Copyright Office in the U.S. Obviously this costs money! A cheaper alternative is to mail a copy of the demo tape or CD, or lead sheet to yourself. Don't open it. Keep it in the sealed envelope in a safe place. Although you will not be registered as the owner of the song, it can help to show when it was written.

Teresa O'Brien
21 Diva Drive
Cork
Ireland

It's a good idea to use some form of recorded delivery when you are mailing your song.

Royalties

Once you have a record deal, you are entitled to royalties from record sales, and from the performance or public broadcast of your song on, for example, TV and radio. To receive royalties, you need to register with a copyright agency. Royalties from record sales are distributed by the Mechanical-Copyright Protection Society (MCPS) in the UK and organizations such as the Harry Fox Agency or the American Society for Composers, Authors and Publishers (ASCAP) in the U.S.A. Performance royalties are collected from clubs, concert venues, shops, and TV and radio stations, by the Performing Rights Society (PRS) in the UK and companies such as Broadcast Music Inc. in the U.S.A. See page 47 for the addresses of all of these organizations.

Below you can find out the names of the notes on a keyboard and how they are written in music notation.

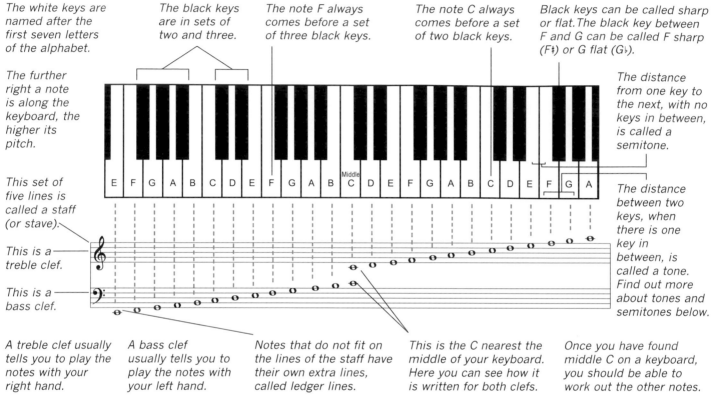

The white keys are named after the first seven letters of the alphabet.

The further right a note is along the keyboard, the higher its pitch.

This set of five lines is called a staff (or stave).

This is a treble clef.

This is a bass clef.

The black keys are in sets of two and three.

The note F always comes before a set of three black keys.

The note C always comes before a set of two black keys.

Black keys can be called sharp or flat. The black key between F and G can be called F sharp (F♯) or G flat (G♭).

The distance from one key to the next, with no keys in between, is called a semitone.

The distance between two keys, when there is one key in between, is called a tone. Find out more about tones and semitones below.

A treble clef usually tells you to play the notes with your right hand.

A bass clef usually tells you to play the notes with your left hand.

Notes that do not fit on the lines of the staff have their own extra lines, called ledger lines.

This is the C nearest the middle of your keyboard. Here you can see how it is written for both clefs.

Once you have found middle C on a keyboard, you should be able to work out the other notes.

Scales

A scale is a sequence of notes going up or down the staff. Most music is based on scales. A scale is named after the note on which it begins. The most common types of scales are major and minor scales. Each type of scale has its own fixed pattern of tones and semitones.

There are two types of minor scale, called harmonic and melodic (see A harmonic and melodic minor scales on the right). In the melodic minor scale, the pattern of tones and semitones varies depending on whether the notes are going up or down.

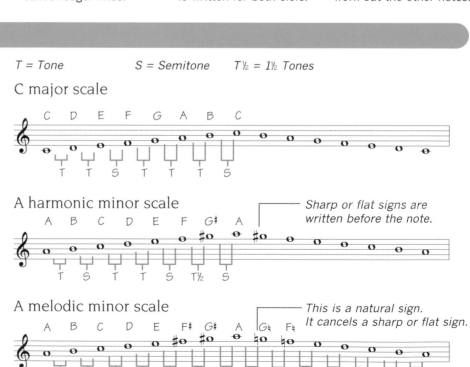

T = Tone   S = Semitone   T½ = 1½ Tones

C major scale

A harmonic minor scale

Sharp or flat signs are written before the note.

A melodic minor scale

This is a natural sign. It cancels a sharp or flat sign.

Keys

A song based around the scale of C major is said to be in the key of C. In some keys there are sharps (♯) or flats (♭) next to the clef. These are called the key signature. They tell you to play these notes sharp or flat throughout a piece.

Minor scales include sharps or flats that do not appear in the key signature. The key signature of a minor scale can be determined by the pattern of tones and semitones in a descending melodic minor.

D major scale

The scale of D major has F sharp and C sharp as its key signature.

You can figure out a scale's key signature by the pattern of tones and semitones.

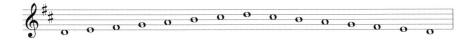
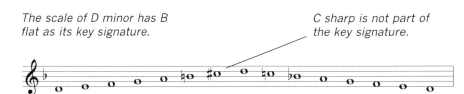

D melodic minor scale

The scale of D minor has B flat as its key signature.

C sharp is not part of the key signature.

Playing chords

Chords are named after the scale on which they are based. They usually consist of the first, third and fifth notes of the scale. Chords are often shown by letters above the music. Here you can see which keys to press to play some of the most common chords.

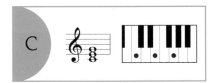

You can play these notes in any order. For example, you might choose to have G as the lowest note, and E as the highest note.

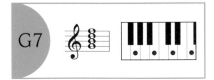

Sometimes an extra note is added 7 notes above the first. This is called a 7th chord.

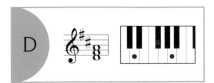

You don't have to play all the notes close together. Try spreading the notes out, leaving a greater distance between each note.

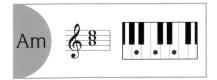

A small m after the chord name means it is minor.

Three-chord sequences

Many songs use only three different chords. Here you can see some groups of three chords that sound good together. You can play these chords in any order. To end a sequence, play the last chord, followed by the first (e.g. in C major, play G then C).

The last chord in each group below can sometimes be a 7th chord. Adding a 7th chord can make the music more interesting.

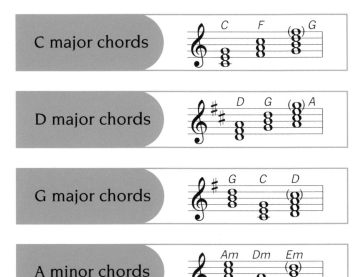

C major chords

D major chords

G major chords

A minor chords

Below you can find out the names of the notes on a guitar and how they are written in music notation.

To find out about scales and keys, go back and read these sections on pages 42 and 43.

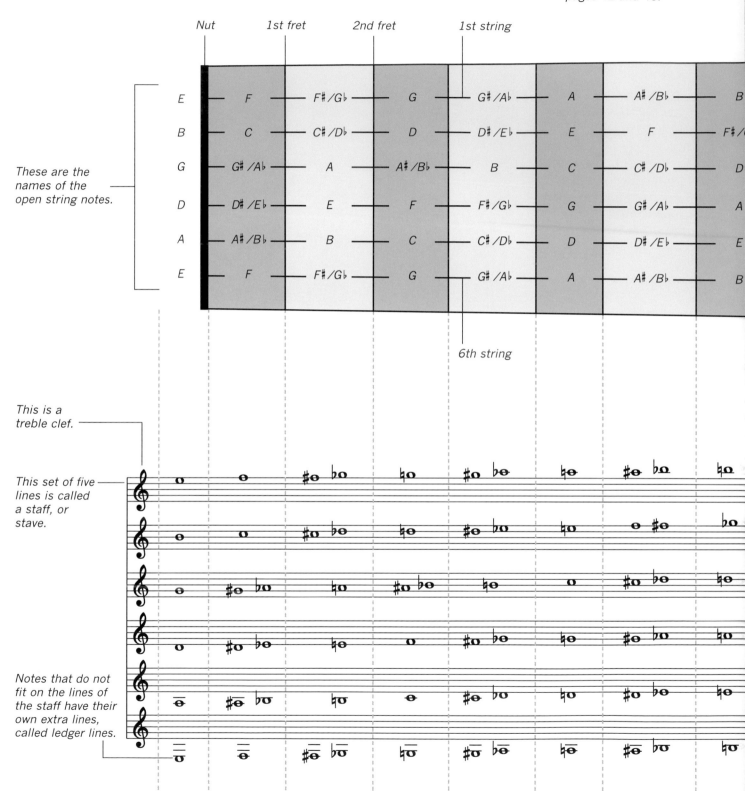

Nut   1st fret   2nd fret   1st string

These are the names of the open string notes.

6th string

This is a treble clef.

This set of five lines is called a staff, or stave.

Notes that do not fit on the lines of the staff have their own extra lines, called ledger lines.

Where two notes are shown on the same fret, these are notes which can be called sharp (♯) or flat (♭).

The distance between each fret is a semitone (see page 42).

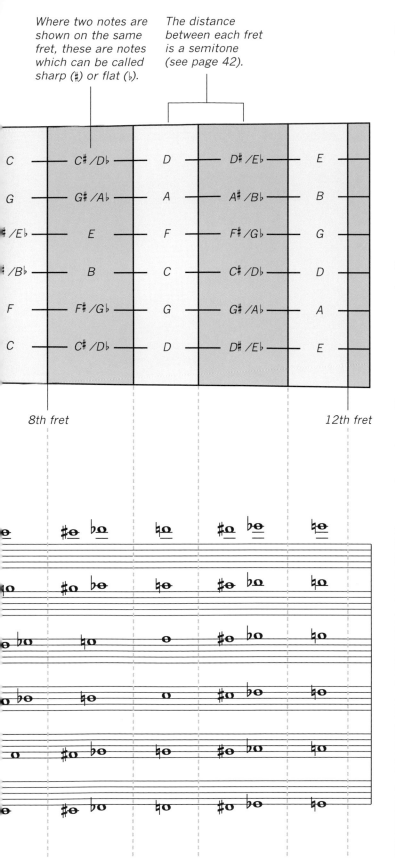

8th fret   12th fret

Tablature

Tablature is another way of writing down guitar music. It uses six lines which represent the strings of a guitar.

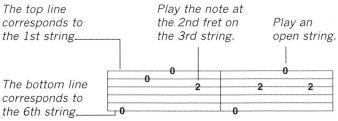

The top line corresponds to the 1st string.

Play the note at the 2nd fret on the 3rd string.

Play an open string.

The bottom line corresponds to the 6th string.

Playing chords

When you play more than one note at a time, it is called playing chords. Chords are often shown by a letter above the staff rather than being written out as notes (see below). The diagrams below show you at which frets to play.

Three-chord sequences

Here are some of the most common chords. They are shown in groups of three. The chords in each group sound good together in any order. To end a sequence, play the last chord followed by the first (eg. in D major, play A then D).

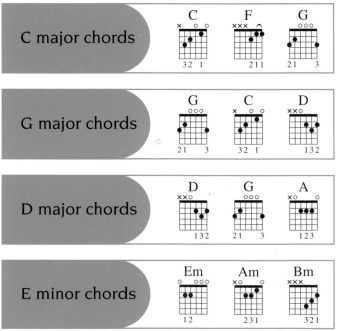

C major chords

G major chords

D major chords

E minor chords

The notes of a melody are usually made up from beats of different lengths. When you write music down, the shape of the note tells you how many beats it lasts for.

Note lengths

Here you can see the most common types of notes and how many beats they last for.

 This is a quarter-note (also known as a crotchet). It lasts for one quarter beat.

 This is a half-note (also known as a minim). It lasts for two quarter beats.

 This is a whole-note (also known as a semibreve). It lasts for four quarter beats.

 A dot after a note makes it half as long again. So a dotted half-note lasts for three quarter beats.

 This is an eighth-note (also known as a quaver). It lasts for half a quarter beat.

Eighth-notes can be joined together like this.

 This is a sixteenth-note (also known as a semiquaver). There are four sixteenth notes in a quarter beat.

Sixteenth-notes can also be joined together.

Rests

A gap in the music is called a rest. You count rests just like notes.

 Quarter rest (one beat)

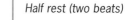 *Half rest (two beats)*

 *Whole rest (four beats)*

Eighth rest (half a beat)

 Sixteenth rest (quarter of a beat)

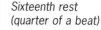 *Dotted quarter rest (one and a half beats)*

Scarborough Fair

Here you can see how notes and rests are written in music.

Tie. *A curved line joining two notes of the same pitch. This makes the first note as long as both notes added together.*

Bar line. *Divides the music into bars.*

Staff, *or* **stave.** *A set of five lines on which music is written.*

Lyrics. *The words of a song are written below the notes.*

Time signature. *Tells you how to count. The top number tells you there are 3 beats in each bar. The bottom number 4 means the beats are quarter notes.*

Hyphen. *Tells you the word is not finished.*

Are you go - ing ___ to Scar(-)bor-ough Fair: ___

Pars-ley, sage, rose-mar-y and thyme. ___

Treble clef. *The clef is written on each staff of a piece.*

Dotted note. *A dot after a note makes it half as long again.*

Key signature. *Tells you to alter the pitch of some notes (see page 43).*

Rest. *Tells you to leave a silence in the music. The shape of the rest tells you how long it lasts for.*

Sharp sign. *This raises the pitch of the note after it by a semitone (see page 42).*

USEFUL ADDRESSES

Send your song to this address to register it in the UK:

The Registrar
Stationers Hall
Ludgate Hill
London EC4M 7DD

Tel: (0171) 248 2934

This company distributes UK broadcasting royalties:

MCPS (Mechanical-Copyright Protection
Society) Ltd
Elgar House
41 Streatham High Road
London SW16 1ER

Tel: (0181) 664 4400
http://www.mcps.co.uk

*This organization collects and distributes
performance royalties in the UK:*

PRS (Performing Rights Society) Ltd,
29-33 Berners Street
London W1P 4AA

Tel: (0171) 580 5544
http://www.prs.co.uk

*Contact this company for information on
British record companies:*

BPI (British Phonographic Industry)
25 Savile Row
London W1X 1AA

Tel: (0171) 287 2252
http://www.bpi.co.uk

*To get help and advice on issues such as
managers, contracts and copyright:*

Musicians' Union
National Office
60/62 Clapham Road
London SW9 0JJ

Tel: (0171) 582 5566
http://www.musiciansunion.org.uk

Send your song here to register it in the U.S.A.:

United States Copyright Office
Library of Congress
101 Independence Avenue
S.E., Washington, D.C.
20559-6000

Tel: (202) 707-3000
http://www.lcweb.loc.gov/copyright

This agency distributes U.S.A. broadcasting royalties:

HFA (Harry Fox Agency)
711 Third Avenue
New York, NY 10017

Tel: (212) 370-5330
http://www.nmpa.org/hfa.html

This society also distributes U.S. broadcasting royalties:

ASCAP (American Society of Composers, Authors
and Publishers)
One Lincoln Place
New York
NY 10023

Tel: (212) 621-6000
http://www.ascap.com

*This organization collects and distributes
performance royalties in the U.S.A.:*

BMI (Broadcast Music Inc.)
320 West 57th Street
New York
NY 10019-3790

Tel: (212) 586-2000
http://www.bmi.com

*Contact this U.S. group for help on choosing managers,
copyright issues and playing live:*

AFM (American Federation of Musicians)
1501 Broadway
Suite 600
New York, NY 10036

Tel: (757) 622-8095
http://www.afm.org

Acknowledgements

The publishers would like to thank the following for the use of their photographic material:
Redferns (cover, Michael Jackson; page 8, Paul Simon; page 13, Kurt Cobain; page 16, Robbie Williams; page 25, Sting; page 31, Burt Bacharach; page 36, Michael Jackson; page 39, George Martin; pages 40-41, audience; page 11, Stevie Wonder). *Rex Features* (pages 3, 14, Madonna; page 12, Janet Jackson; page 15, Andrew Lloyd Webber; page 17, Keith Richards and Mick Jagger; page 22, The Artist; page 29, Abba). *Getty Images* (page 6, Bob Dylan). *Pictorial Press Ltd.* (cover, Kurt Cobain; page 4, Paul McCartney and John Lennon; page 18, Jimi Hendrix; page 19, Carole King; page 24, Kurt Weill; page 26, Charles Trenet). *Archive Photos* (page 35, Jacques Brel).

Retna Pictures Ltd. (cover, Björk and Lauryn Hill; page 5, Elton John and Bernie Taupin; page 9, Björk; page 21, David Bowie; page 30, Noel Gallagher; page 32, Sheryl Crow). *Big Bang Productions*, P.O. Box 88, Loleta, Humboldt County, California, 95551, Tel: 707 733 5778, **http://www.bigbangpr.com**, email: **info@bigbangpr.com** (page 38, recording studio); *Helwett Packard Ltd.* (page 5, computer). The publishers wish to thank the following for supplying the instruments used in the photos: Fender Musical Instruments Corporation; Digital Village, London; Yamaha-Kemble Music (UK) Ltd; Thanks to JoMoX, Germany, for creating the easy-to-use XBase09, the real analog drum machine. The songwriter's hands in the photos are those of Sarah Cronin.